VINTAGE COMMERCIAL
ART & DESIGN

FRANK H. ATKINSON | CHARLES J. STRONG | L. S. STRONG

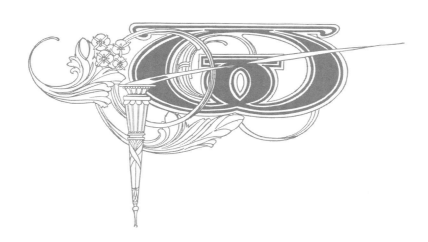

DOVER PUBLICATIONS, INC.
MINEOLA, NEW YORK

Bibliographical Note

This Dover edition, first published in 2011, contains a selection of images from *Sign Painting* by Frank H. Atkinson (1915) and *Strong's Book of Designs* (1917) both originally published by Frederick J. Drake & Company, Chicago.

DOVER *Pictorial Archive* SERIES

International Standard Book Number
ISBN-13: 978-0-486-47845-6
ISBN-10: 0-486-47845-9

Manufactured in the United States by Courier Corporation
47845901
www.doverpublications.com

Note

This exquisite collection of commercial signs, images, and fonts are from two rare, early-twentieth century sources that were used as a reference for sign painters and lithographers. This valuable resource includes over 1,400 eye-catching signs and design elements—including 25 different fonts and over 100 full-color images! Ranging from elegant and delicate to big and bold, these timeless images will inspire artists, craftspeople, or anybody who wants to add a classic vintage accent to their work.

The "Images" folder on the CD contains two folders. All of the high-resolution JPEG files have been placed in one folder and all of the Internet-ready JPEG images can be found in the other folder. Every image has a unique file name in the following format: xxx.JPG. The first 3 digits of the file name, before the period, correspond to the number printed under the image in the book. The last 3 letters of the file name "JPG," refer to the file format. So, 001.JPG would be the first file in the folder.

Also included on the CD-ROM is Dover Design Manager, a simple graphics editing program for Windows that will allow you to view, print, crop, and rotate the images.

For technical support, contact:
    Telephone: 1 (617) 249-0245
    Fax: 1 (617) 249-0245
    Email: dover@artimaging.com
    Internet: http://www.dovertechsupport.com
    The fastest way to receive technical support is via email or the Internet.

0001

0002

ECCENTRIC

PANELS

A customer that gets the **"BUTT-END"** of a deal goes straight up and **NEVER COMES BACK!**

WE HAVE NO "STRONG BUTTER"

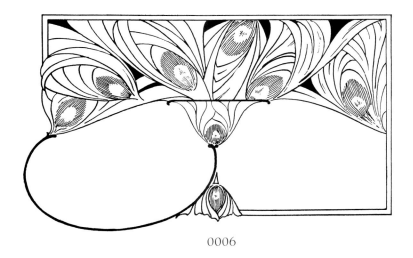

0006

0007

Pen and Ink work

0008

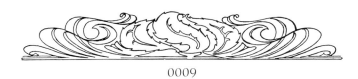

0009

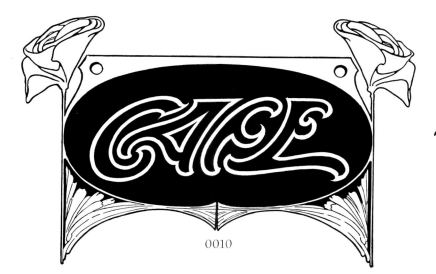

0010

0011

Splash with me at

PLEASURE PARK

Thur. the 4th

The "Bunch" will be there

Round Trip fifty cents

Good Music ♪

There & Back Ten Cents.

SKATING at Belle Isle

BULLETIN & DESIGNS

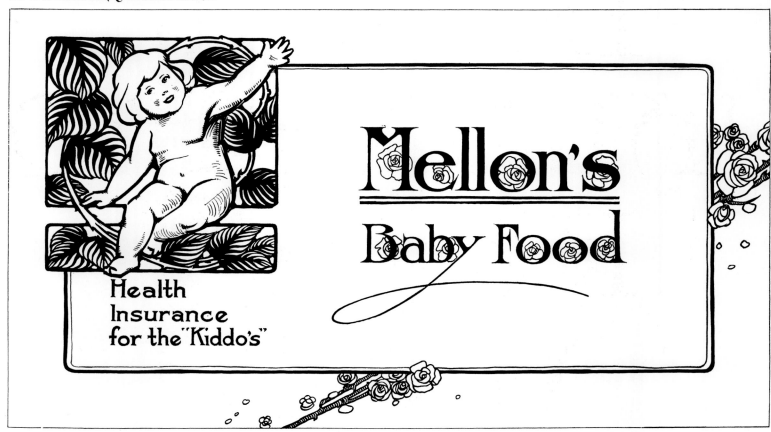

Health
Insurance
for the "Kiddo's"

Mellon's
Baby Food

0014

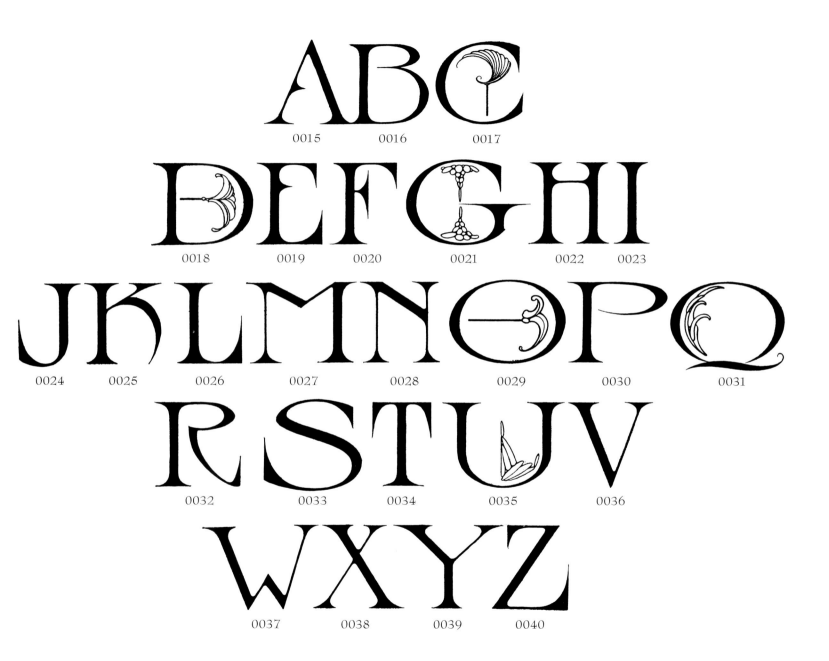

ABC
0015 0016 0017

DEFGHI
0018 0019 0020 0021 0022 0023

JKLMNOPQ
0024 0025 0026 0027 0028 0029 0030 0031

RSTUV
0032 0033 0034 0035 0036

WXYZ
0037 0038 0039 0040

9

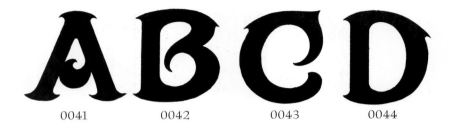

0041 0042 0043 0044

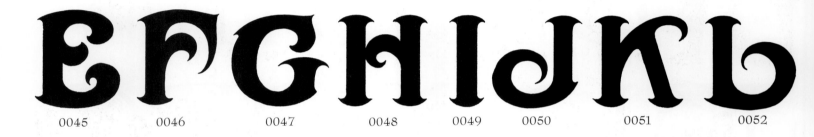

0045 0046 0047 0048 0049 0050 0051 0052

0053 0054 0055 0056 0057 0058 0059

U V W X Y Z

0060 0061 0062 0063 0064 0065

0066 0067 0068

0069 0070 0071 0072 0073 0074 0075

0076 0077 0078 0079 0080 0081 0082

0083 0084 0085 0086 0087

0088 0089 0090 0091 0092

11

PHONE
Black 925

209
ALDER
ST.

FredWatrin
Sign Painter

Portland Or.

0093

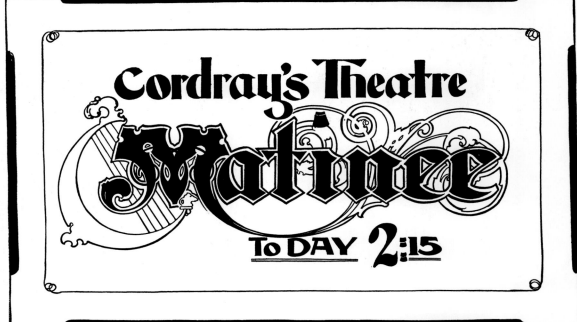

Cordray's Theatre
Matinee
To Day 2:15

0094

0095   0096   0097   0098

0099   0100   0101   0102   0103   0104   0105

0106   0107   0109   0110   0111   0112

0108

0113   0114   0115   0116   0117   0118

ABCDEFG
0119 0120 0121 0122 0123 0124 0125

HIJKLMN
0126 0127 0128 0129 0130 0131 0132

OPRSTUV
0133 0134 0135 0136 0137 0138 0139

WXYZ
0140 0141 0142 0143 0144 0145

1234567890
0146 0147 0148 0149 0150 0151 0152 0153 0154

14

A·R·HUSSEY

Designer   Man'frer

SIGNS

0155

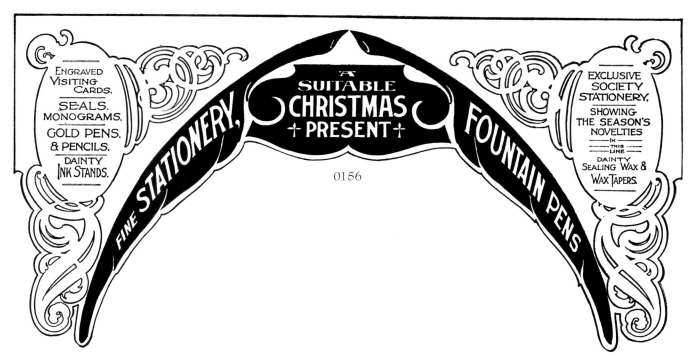

ENGRAVED
VISITING
CARDS.

SEALS.
MONOGRAMS.

GOLD PENS.
& PENCILS.

DAINTY
INK STANDS.

A
SUITABLE
CHRISTMAS
✦ PRESENT ✦

FINE STATIONERY,

FOUNTAIN PENS

EXCLUSIVE
SOCIETY
STATIONERY.

SHOWING
THE SEASON'S
NOVELTIES
IN
THIS
LINE

DAINTY
SEALING WAX &
WAX TAPERS.

0156

Sporting Goods
7th Floor.

0157

16

A B G D

0158   0159   0160   0161

0162   0163   0164   0165   0166   0167   0168   0169

0170   0171   0173   0174   0175   0176

0172

0177   0178   0179   0180   0181   0182

17

IMPORTED AND DOMESTIC

FOR THE HOLIDAYS

CIGARS

CIGARETTES.

PIPES AND SMOKERS ARTICLES.

0183

HEADQUARTERS FOR

TOYS

FOR XMAS

IMPORTED NOVELTIES.

0184

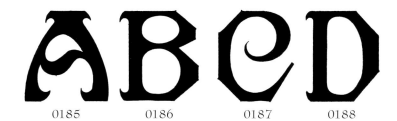

0185   0186   0187   0188

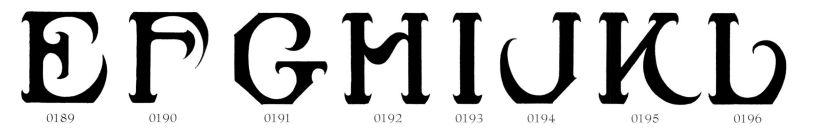

0189   0190   0191   0192   0193   0194   0195   0196

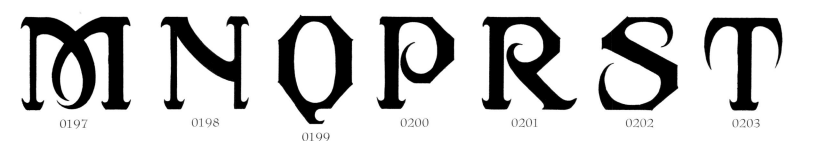

0197   0198   0199   0200   0201   0202   0203

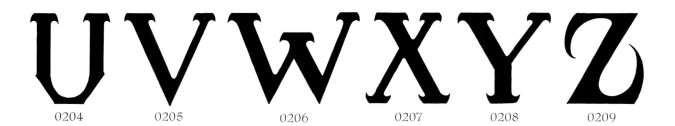

0204   0205   0206   0207   0208   0209

AN ARTISTIC GIFT

Teco

ART POTTERY.

FOR XMAS

0210

OLD & RARE VOLUMES.

YULE-TIDE OFFERINGS

BOOKS

Complete Editions Of Popular Authors.

0211

H·C·
BODER,
SIGN
PAINTER
PHONE
SO-512.

0212

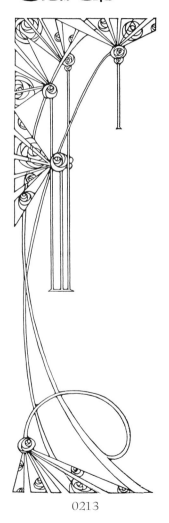

Business Cards

0213

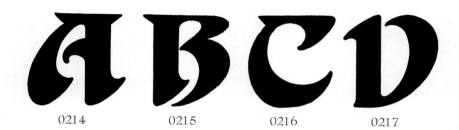

0214   0215   0216   0217

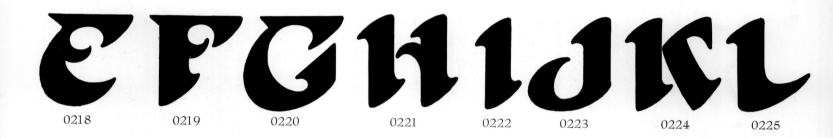

0218   0219   0220   0221   0222   0223   0224   0225

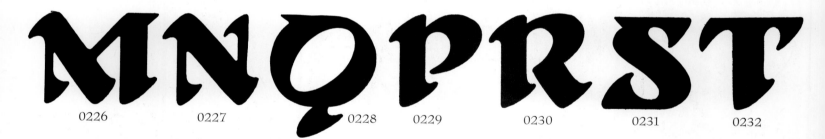

0226   0227   0228   0229   0230   0231   0232

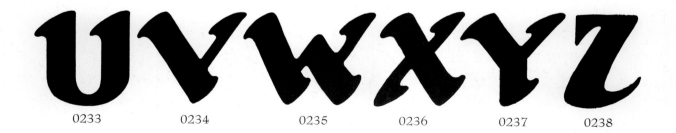

0233   0234   0235   0236   0237   0238

0239   0240   0241   0242   0243   0244   0245

0246   0247   0248   0249   0250   0251   0252   0253   0254

0255   0256   0257   0258   0259   0260   0261   0262

0263   0264   0265   0266   0267   0268

0269 0270 0271 0272 0273 0274 0275 0276 0277 0278 0279 0280 0281 0282 0283 0284

0285 0286 0288 0289 0290 0291 0292 0293 0294 0295 0296 0297 0298 0299
0287

·I·B·
PERRY
·CO·

SIGNS

0300

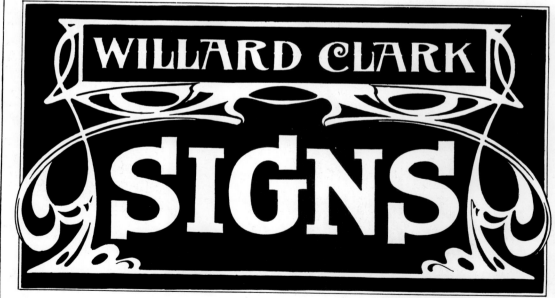

WILLARD CLARK

SIGNS

0301

0302

0303

C.S. FORINGTON CO.

COMMERCIAL

SIGN PAINTERS

BANK AND OFFICE LETTERING.

0304

"All Sports" are enjoying

No "dope" No flavoring

THE "Referee"

THE NEW 5¢ CIGAR

0305

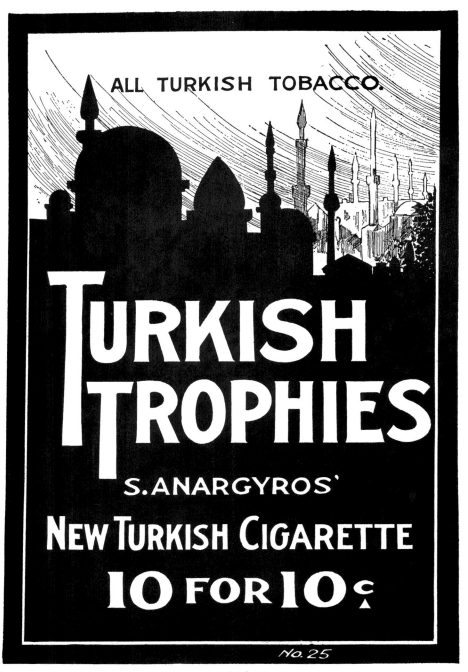

0306

0307

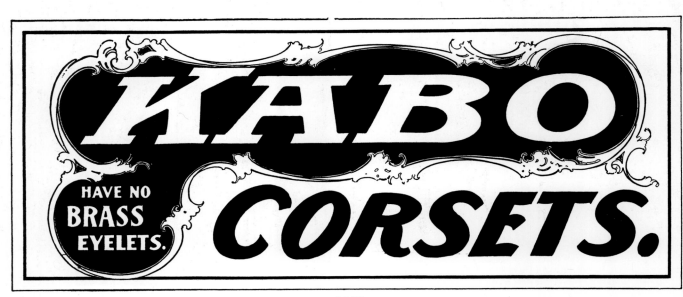

0308

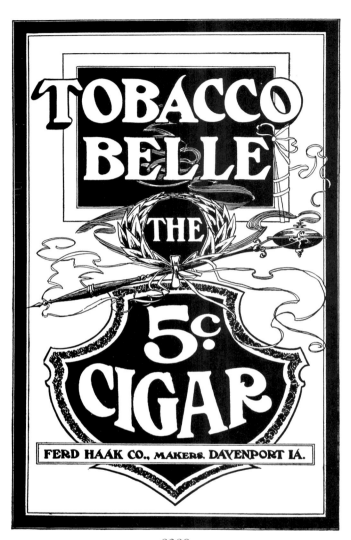

0309

0310

0311

0312

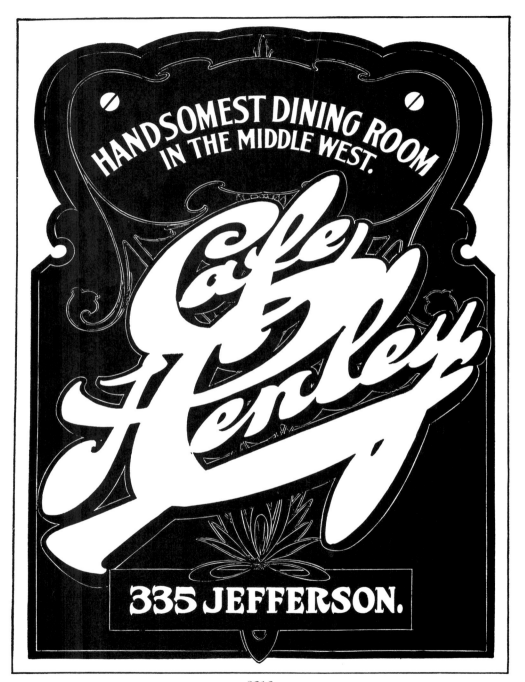

0313

0314

0315

0316

0317

0318

0319

0320

·PHONE YARDS 1306·

CENTRAL DISPLAY CO

ADVERTISING & COMMERCIAL SIGN PAINTERS.

768 Thirty First St.

0321

THE
MILLINERY
IMPORTING
CO.

0322

0323

0324

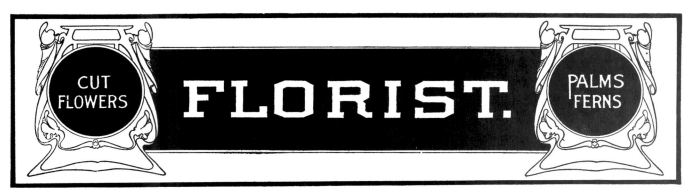

0325

Grant's Printery

PRINTING

CATALOGS
BOOKLETS

Job & 27 Society

POSTERS
FOLDERS

PHONE SO. 1236.

0326

RESTAURANT

FOR
LADIES
AND GENTLEMEN.

0327

0328

0329

0330

0331

0332

0333

44

ESTABLISHED 1870.

ALLAWAY & HANCOX

SIGNS

2540=2542
COTTAGE
GROVE
AV.

PHONE SO. 1058.

SIGN HANGING.

CHICAGO.

0334

A RAG TIME STUNT IN

SIGNS

THE HELLO KIND.

0335

0336

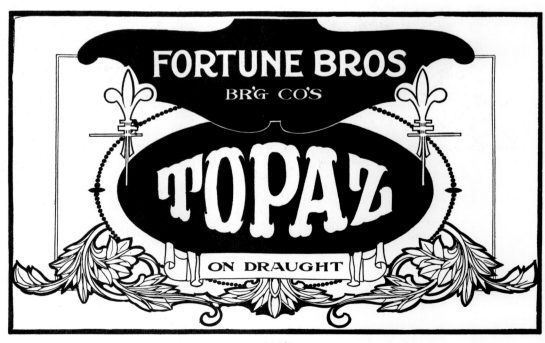

0337

RAVINIA PARK

OPEN AIR
VAUDEVILLE

50 ARTISTS 50

AFTERNOON
AND
EVENING

0338

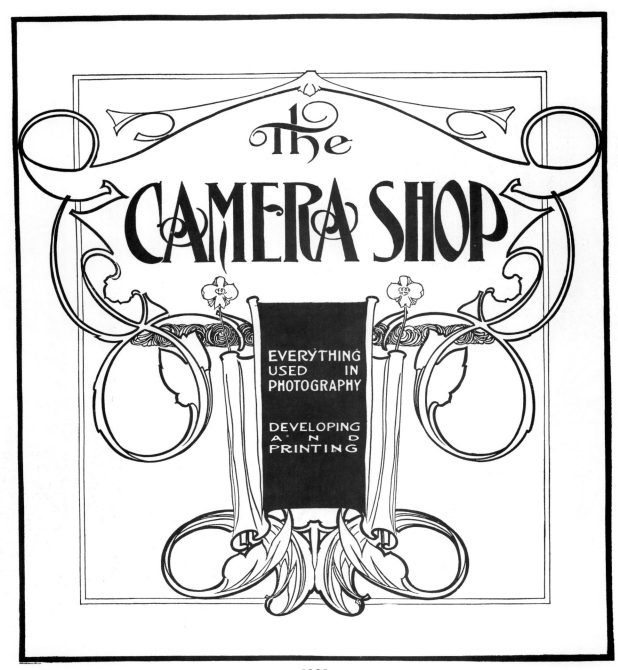

The

CAMERA SHOP

EVERYTHING
USED IN
PHOTOGRAPHY

DEVELOPING
A N D
PRINTING

0340

TAKE YELLOW CARS

BATHING

Direct to
ASTORIA
BEACH

BOATING

WATER POLO

AQUATIC SPORTS

REGATTA EVERY SATURDAY P.M.

0341

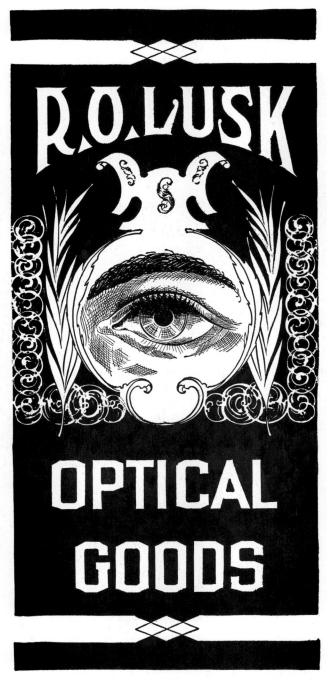

0342

0343

Royal Dentifrice

That gleam of white behind the lips that gives the smile it's chiefest beauty, milady cleans and here's the means that add a pleasure to the duty.

0344

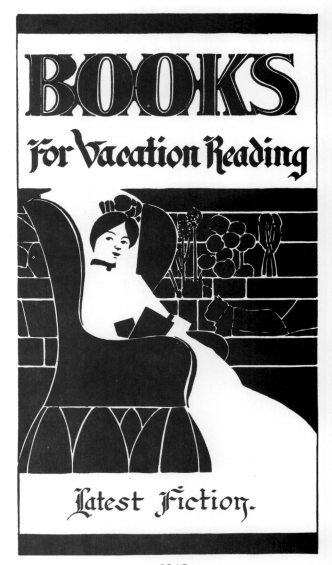

BOOKS
for Vacation Reading

Latest Fiction.

0345

52

Exhibition Of Black and White Drawings by Jessie M. King.

Bruton Galleries 13 Bruton Street.

Open Daily 10 to 6

Catalogues

0346

ABCDEFGHIJ
KLMNOPQRST
UVWXYZ&
ES
abcdefghijklmnopqrst
uvwxyz 123456789

0347–0410

FRENCH ROMAN

A

CD   I   a

BEF   234   dcb

GHIJK   5   efg

LMNOPOR   6   hijlmnok

STUV   7   prstq

WXY   89   uv

w

0411–0435   0436–0444   0445–0467

Coliseum Garden

Every Night at 8.
Ferullo,
Conductor:

Ellerys
Band.

0468

0469

56

Ye Olde Inn Ale

The ale of "Olde England" brewed in America
and superior to any other imported, other domestic.

One Dozen Bottles $1.50

Keeley Brewing Co.

On Draught
Ask the Bar-Man.

0470

ATKINSON TUSCAN ROMAN (Light)

A B C D E F G
H I J K L M O P
Q R S T U V W
X Y Z
&
0471–0496

FRENCH ROMAN (LIGHT)

A
BC
DEF
GHIJK
LMNOPQR
STUV
WXY
Z
&

0507–0533

4123
956
78
O

0497–0506

a
dcb
efg
hijlmnok
pstq
uv
w
xy
z

0534–0558

59

0559

Extreme French

ABCDFGHIJKLMNOPQ
RSTUVWXYZ&E
a   12 34 567 89   WYXZ
abcdefgfhijklmnoopqrsstuv

0560–0625

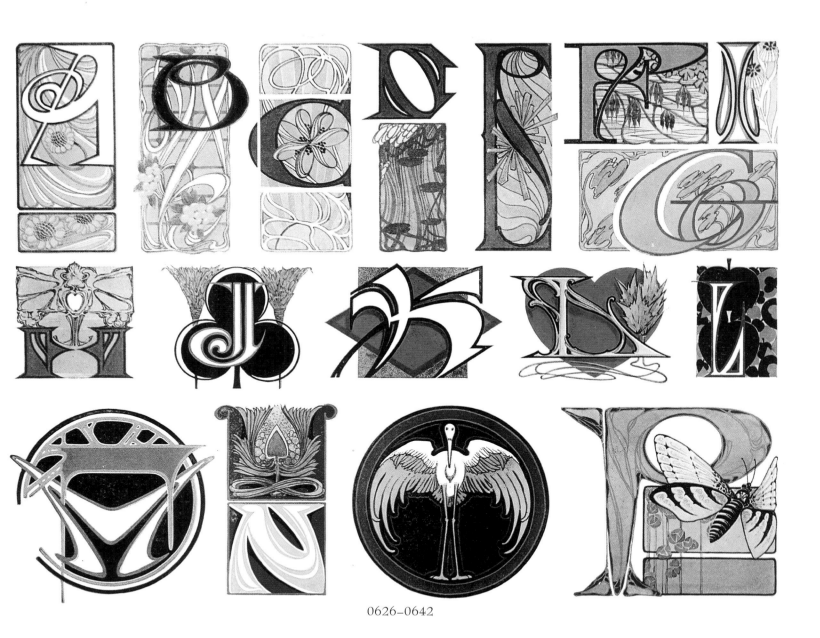

0626–0642

0643

0644

0645

0646

0647

0648

0649

0650

0651

0652

0653

0654

0655

0656

0657

0658

0659

0660

0661

0662

0663

0664

0665

0666

0667

0668

0669

0670

0671

0672

0673

0674

Peculiar Decoration.

0675

0676

0677

0678

0679

65

Odds and Ends

0680

0681

0682

1910

Practical Ornamentation

0683

0684

0685

0686

0687

0688

0689

0690

0691

0692

0693

0694

0695

HANDY IDEAS

0696

0697

0698

0699

0700

0701

0702

0703

0704

0705

0706

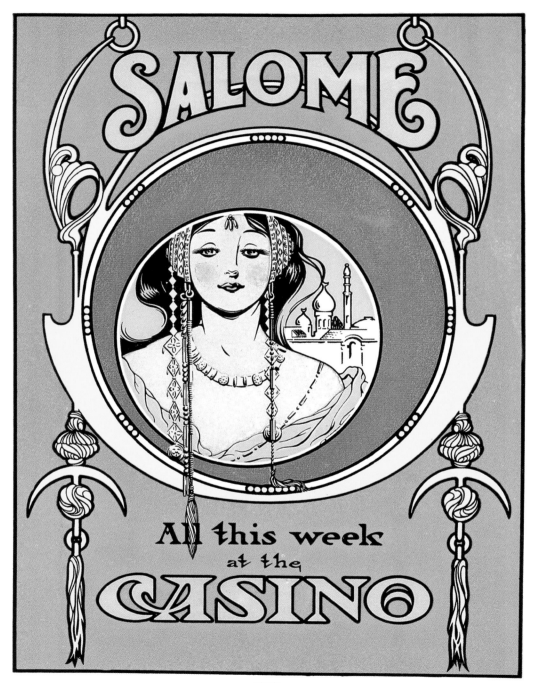

0707

RIBBONS

0708

0709

0710

0711 0712 0713 0714

72

0715

0716

0717

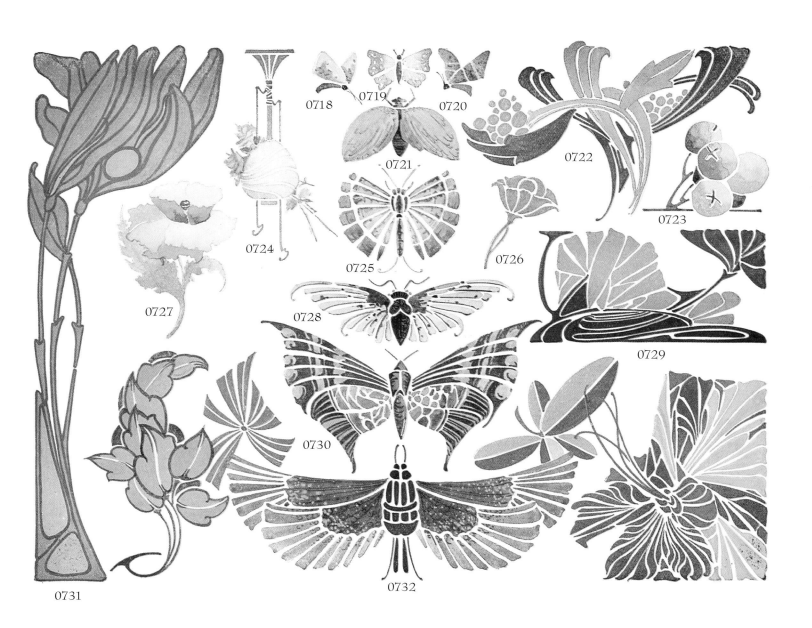

0718

0719

0720

0721

0722

0723

0724

0725

0726

0727

0728

0729

0730

0731

0732

SHOW CARDS

Buffalo N.Y.

0733

NOTHING TO IT —

Taking Care of a

CADILLAC

ALL ROADS LOOK ALIKE TO ME.

CADILLAC MOTOR CAR CO.
Detroit, Mich.

0734

FAIRMONT GAS COAL

0735

0736

0737

0738

0739

0740

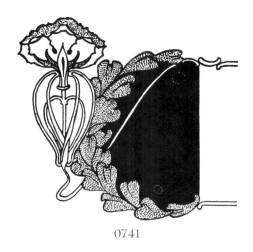

0741

0742

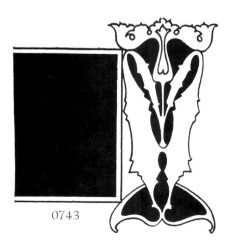

0743

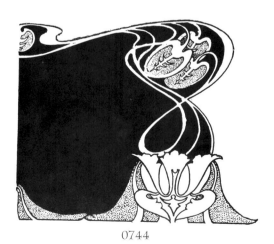

0744

0745

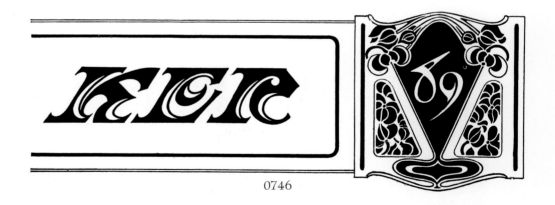

0746

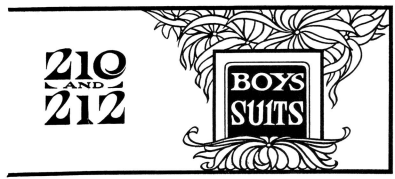

0747

0748

0749

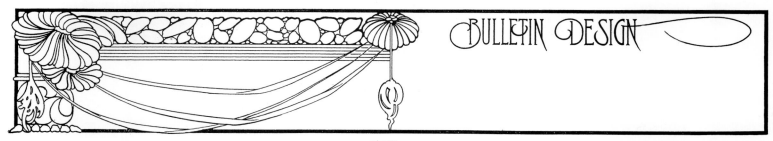

0750

Things Vncommon

0752

0753

Tablet Design.

0754

WATCHES, JEWELRY, DIAMONDS

HOLIDAY GIFTS

FINE SELECTION, RELIABLE IN EVERY WAY.

0755

0756

0757

0758

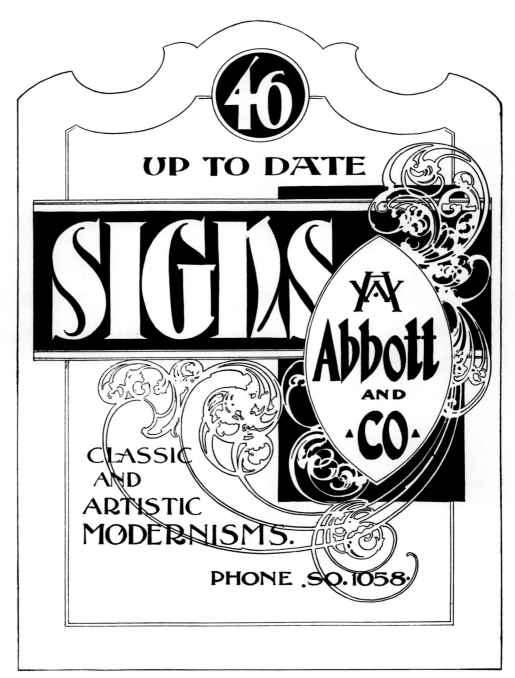

46

UP TO DATE

SIGNS

ﾔﾔ
Abbott
AND
·CO·

CLASSIC
AND
ARTISTIC
MODERNISMS.

PHONE ·SO·1058·

0759

Eccentric French

ABCCDEFFGJHIKLM
NQPRSTUVWXYZ&
acbdefghijkmnoprstuvwxyz
F SSE SS & & & L EE L
SE E L L C E NAMES

0761–0838

Heavy Sign Script

ABCDEFGHIJKLMNO2
PRSUVWXYZ

0839–0863

92

Show Card French

ABCDEFGHIJKLMN
OPQRSTUVWXY
Z&
aabcdefghijklmnopqr
aaſ xyſtuvwz g ſ w
I 3245678 9 ₃

0864–0934

After
you have used
Sanitol

Your teeth will gleam like Ivory and your breath will have the delicate fragrance of the rose.

The Sanitol Co.

0935

0936

0937

0938

0939

ABCDEFG
NOPQRST
1234567 8Z

efghijklmnopr

0940–1001

HIJKLM
UVWXY
90&abcd
stuvwxyz

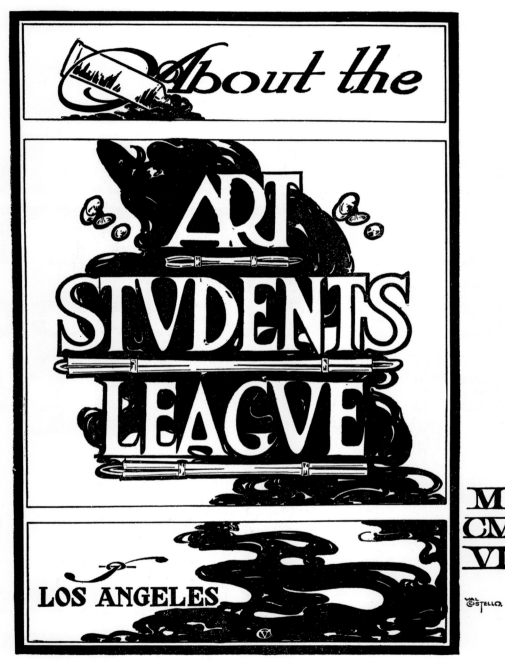

About the

ART STVDENTS LEAGVE

LOS ANGELES

MCMVI

1002

1003

1004

102

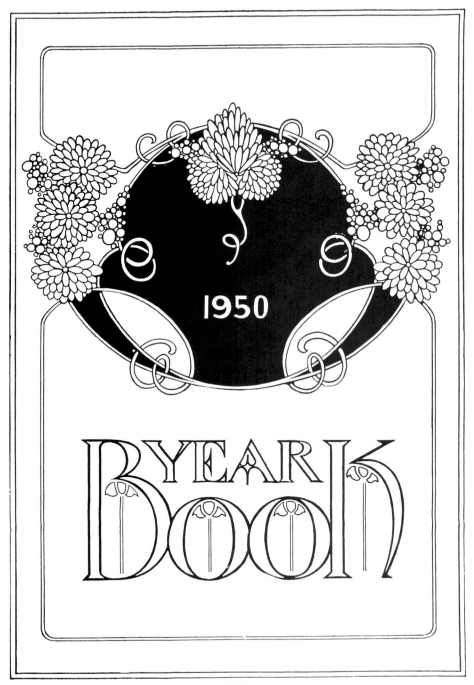

1950

YEAR BOOK

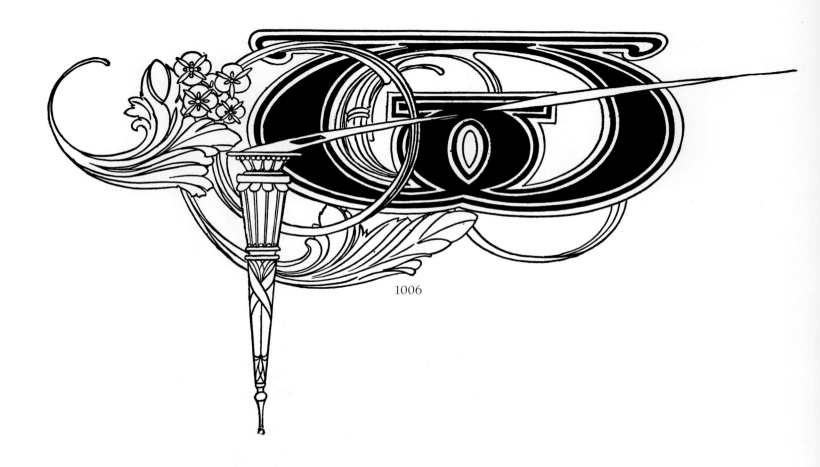

1006

HOLIDAY SIGNS ON OIL CLOTH·MUSLIN· Etc.

1008

1009

1010

ABCDEFGH
PQRSTUV
abcdefghijk
stuvwxyz 12

1011–1072

HALF·CLASSIC·ROMAN·

IJKLMNO
WXYZ&
lmnopqr
3456789

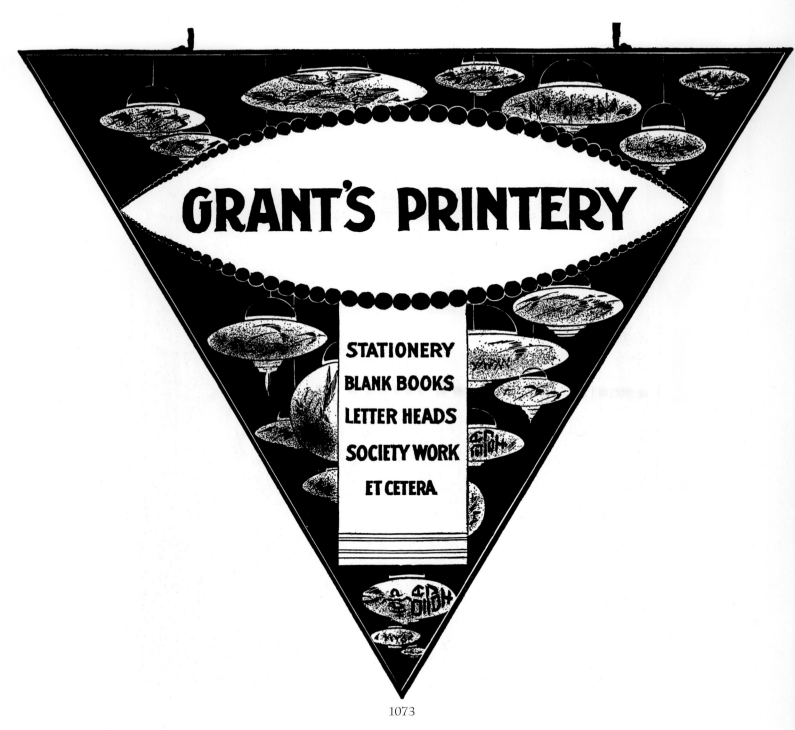

GRANT'S PRINTERY

STATIONERY
BLANK BOOKS
LETTER HEADS
SOCIETY WORK
ET CETERA

1073

1074

ABCDEFGHIJKLMNO
PQRSTUVWXYZ&123
456789abcdefghijkl
mnopqrstuvxwzy

1075–1136

MODIFIED TUSCAN ROMAN

ABCDEFGHIJKLMNOPQR
STUVWXYZ&123456789
abcdefghijklmnopqrstuvwxyz

ALTERNATIVES CEFGJS EE
EESFT ALTERNATIVES

1137–1211

ABCDEFGHIJKLM
NOPQRSTUVW
&XYZ&

abcdefghijklmnopqr
sutvwxyz
1234567890

1212–1275

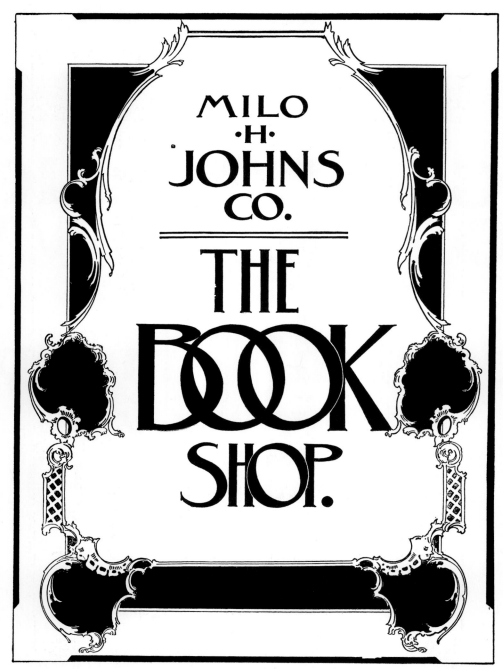

MILO
·H·
JOHNS
CO.

THE
BOOK
SHOP.

1276

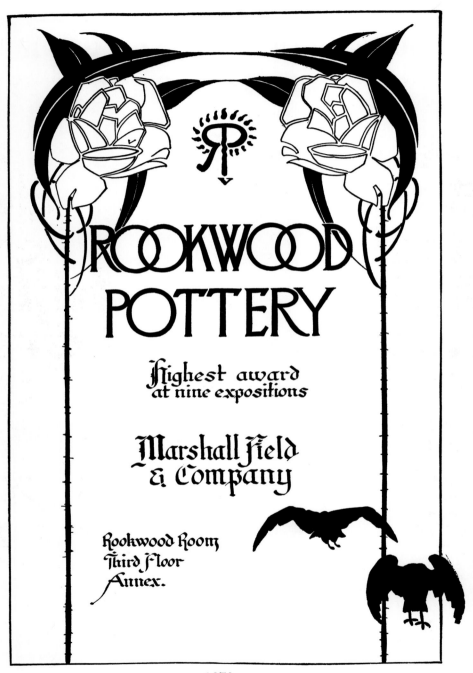

ROOKWOOD POTTERY

Highest award
at nine expositions

Marshall Field
& Company

Rookwood Room
Third Floor
Annex.

1278

"ADVERTISERS" "THICK & THIN PLUG"

A

B C

D E F

G H I J K

L M N O P O R

S T U V

W X Y

Z

&

1279–1305

I

2 3

4

5

6

7 8

9

1306–1314

a

d c b

e f g

h i j l m n o k

q r s t p

u v

w

x y

z

1315–1340

117

ABCDEFGHIJKLM
NOPQRTUVWXY
Z&

abcdefghijklmnopqr
stuvwxyz
123456789

1341–1401

William Daniels,

BREEDER OF

White Wiandottes

STOCK FOR SALE
EGGS IN SEASON.

438 Nelson St.,
CHICAGO.

1402

1403

1404

(heavy) FRENCH ROMAN

A 24567 a

BG 319 dcb

DEF R efg

GHIJK hijlmnok

LMNOPQR R qstp

STUV uv

WXY 8 R w sp

Z ER xy

& z

1405–1431   1432–1445   1446–1471